Why Science Matters

Pregnancy and Birth

Ann Fullick

Heinemann Library
Chicago, Illinois

Printed and bound in China by Leo Paper Group.

13 12 11 10 09
10 9 8 7 6 5 4 3 2 1

Library of Congress Cataloging-in-Publication Data
Fullick, Ann, 1956-
Pregnancy and birth / Ann Fullick.
    p. cm. -- (Why science matters)
Includes bibliographical references and index.
ISBN 978-1-4329-2479-9 (hc) -- ISBN 978-1-4329-2486-7 (pb)
1. Pregnancy. 2. Childbirth. I. Title.
RG551.F85 2008
618.2--dc22
                    2008051114

Acknowledgments
The author and publishers are grateful to the following for permission to reproduce copyright material:
© Alamy pp. **4**, **11**, **26**, **45**; © Corbis pp. **5** (Pat Doyle), **7** (Michael & Patricia Fogden), **18** (Frederic Larson/
San Francisco Chronicle), **19** (San Francisco Chronicle/Lea Suzuki), **20** (Dung Vo Trung), **30** (Reuters), **46**
(Patricia McDonough); © Istockphoto background images and design features; © Lana Langlois p. **17**
(Dreamstime.com); © Mirrorpix p. **43**; © Photodisc pp. **20** (Jim Wehtje), **29**; © Photolibrary pp. **17** (OSF/
Neil Bromhal), **23** (Blend/Larry Williams), **31** (Phototake Science/Yoav Levy); © Photolibrary Group p. **25**
(Phototake Science); © Science Photo Library pp. **12**, **15**, **22**, **28**, **33**, **34**, **36**, **38**, **44** (Dorling Kindersley/
Ruth Jenkinson); © Rex Features p. **41**.

Cover photograph of nurse with newborn babies reproduced with permission of © Corbis/Waltraud Grubitzsch/dpa.

Every effort has been made to contact copyright holders of any material reproduced in this book. Any omissions
will be rectified in subsequent printings if notice is given to the publisher.

Contents

How Does Reproduction Work? 4

Conception and Pregnancy..................... 12

Maintaining a Healthy Pregnancy 22

Genetic Inheritance................................ 28

Giving Birth 32

Fertility Problems................................... 36

Ethical Issues Surrounding IVF............... 40

Taking Care of the Baby 44

Facts and Figures.................................. 48

Find Out More 52

Glossary.. 54

Index 56

Some words are printed in bold, **like this**. You can find out what they mean in the glossary.

How Does Reproduction Work?

A new baby is usually a cause for celebration. However, childbirth is still a major cause of death in young women, and can also be dangerous for the baby. In many countries, the risks are relatively small because advances in modern science have made childbirth safer than it was in the past. Yet for the millions of women who do not get good medical care during pregnancy and delivery, having a baby is still risky.

Reproduction matters

Pregnancy and childbirth are vital for the human race to continue. All living things need to reproduce (make more of themselves) because otherwise they would become extinct. In this book you will study how people produce babies and try to ensure those babies are as healthy as possible.

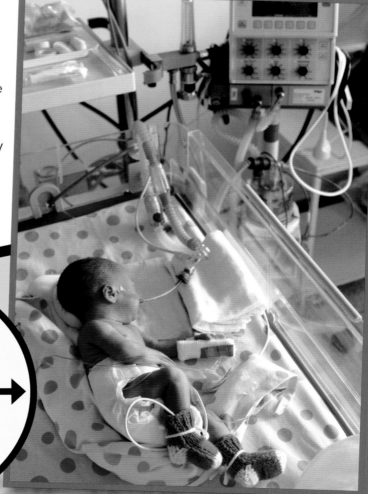

This baby is being cared for in an intensive care unit. Birth is the end of a long and dangerous journey for mother and child.

Types of reproduction

There are two basic methods of reproduction used by all living organisms—**asexual reproduction** and **sexual reproduction**.

Asexual reproduction involves just one parent. Bacteria, many plants, and some simple animals reproduce in this way. All offspring produced by asexual reproduction are identical to their parent—there is no variety. If conditions change (for example, if a new disease appears) all of the identical offspring are equally able, or unable, to cope. This means they could all be wiped out.

Sexual reproduction is usual in more complex animals and plants. It involves two parents and the joining of two special sex cells, known as **gametes**, to form a new, unique individual. This method of reproduction introduces variety, so some of the offspring have a better chance of survival if conditions change. However, it is more risky because the animals and plants have to make sure that the gametes get together. Also, sexual reproduction often requires more investment (commitment) by at least one of the parents. For example, a baby mammal grows inside the body of its mother and needs care once it is born.

This litter of kittens are all different. They show how offspring produced by sexual reproduction can vary.

THE SCIENCE YOU LEARN: GAMETES

Male and female sex cells are called gametes. The female sex cells (eggs in animals, ovules in plants) are usually "few, fat, and fixed": there are not many of them; they are quite large, since they contain food for the **embryo**; and they cannot move by themselves. Male sex cells (sperm in animals, pollen in plants) are usually "many, mini, and mobile": there are lots of them; they are very small; and they can move themselves toward the female gamete.

Animal antics

Animals have developed amazing ways of making sure that their babies survive. Some of these involve adaptations of the body, while others involve specialized behavior.

Many fish and amphibians simply release their eggs and sperm into the water, hoping that the two will meet. Others take a more sophisticated approach. Some fish make nests, which the male lures the female onto to lay her eggs, and then fertilizes immediately with his sperm.

Birds often go to great lengths to produce healthy offspring. The parents mate (the sperm meet the eggs within the body of the female), and the eggs are laid in a nest they have built. The eggs are full of food for the developing baby bird and are covered in a hard protective shell. The parents sit on the eggs and keep them warm for up to several weeks, until the young birds hatch. The parents often feed and take care of their offspring after they hatch until they are grown and independent.

An amazing journey

Marsupials are mammals—but just barely. Like other mammals, the marsupial's egg and sperm meet inside the body of the mother where the embryo begins to develop. Unlike other mammals, marsupials are very tiny and not fully developed when they are born. The Australian red kangaroo, for example, can grow to be 1.6 m (5.2 ft.) tall and weigh roughly 70 kg (150 lbs). Yet the newborn baby kangaroo (known as a joey) is only 2 cm (0.8 in.) long and weighs less than 1 g (0.04 oz.)! As soon as it is born, the tiny joey sets out on an amazing journey through its mother's fur to the inside of her pouch. There it latches onto one of four teats, which supplies the milk it needs to grow. About nine months later, the fully formed joey starts to leave the pouch for increasing amounts of time, but continues to come back to suckle until it is at least one year old. A female kangaroo can have up to three babies at one time: one that has just left her pouch; one developing in her pouch; and an embryo inside her reproductive system ready to move into the pouch when it is empty!

Strawberry poison frog

These tiny, poisonous frogs make great efforts to care for their young. The female frog lays her eggs in small batches on the rain forest floor and the male fertilizes them. For the next week, the male and the female return regularly to keep the eggs moist until the tadpoles start to hatch. When they do, the female carries the hatching tadpoles on her back and places each one in a water-filled hole in a tree, or in the center of a bromeliad (a family of plants that includes the pineapple). The female then returns regularly to where she left each tadpole and lays an infertile egg. This egg provides the tadpole with food. The female does this until the tadpole turns into a froglet and can explore and feed itself.

These little frogs put a lot of effort into raising their young successfully.

Reproduction in humans

People reproduce sexually. A sperm from a man must join with an egg cell from a woman to begin a new human life. For reproduction to be successful, the bodies of men and women need to be very different. These differences are not obvious in very young people. The external sex organs of baby boys and girls are different, but apart from that, babies, toddlers, and young children look very similar. This continues for many years until they enter **puberty**.

During puberty, sex hormones (special chemical messages) start to be produced in the brain and in special glands. These are then carried around the body in the blood. A young person's body goes through many changes as the result of puberty and finally becomes an adult's body, capable of reproduction.

Puberty in boys

The male sex hormone is **testosterone**. When a boy's body is exposed to this hormone he goes into puberty. His reproductive organs mature and become active, and his body changes in a number of ways. The order of the changes varies from one individual to another but usually consists of:

- a big growth spurt causing him to get much taller
- his larynx changing, causing his voice to squeak before becoming deeper
- his shoulders getting broader and his muscles larger
- hair growing on his body and facial hair beginning to appear
- his sex organs growing.

Perhaps the most important change of all is that the production of live sperm begins in the testes. The sperm are produced constantly from puberty onward, often continuing right to the end of a man's life. The testes also make a nutrient-rich fluid that carries the sperm. This mixture of sperm and fluid is known as **semen**.

THE SCIENCE YOU LEARN:
THE MALE REPRODUCTIVE SYSTEM

The male reproductive system involves a complex series of tubes and glands that produce semen. The urethra (the tube that passes through the penis) carries urine from the bladder during urination and semen from the reproductive system during ejaculation. A valve prevents both from being released at the same time.

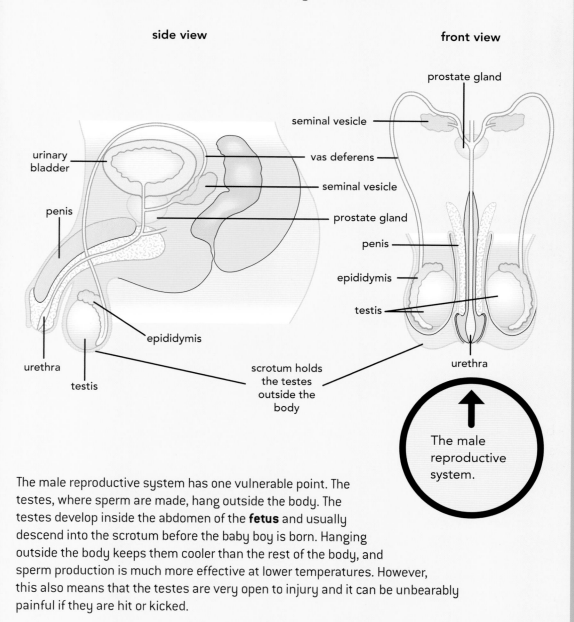

side view

front view

The male reproductive system.

The male reproductive system has one vulnerable point. The testes, where sperm are made, hang outside the body. The testes develop inside the abdomen of the **fetus** and usually descend into the scrotum before the baby boy is born. Hanging outside the body keeps them cooler than the rest of the body, and sperm production is much more effective at lower temperatures. However, this also means that the testes are very open to injury and it can be unbearably painful if they are hit or kicked.

Puberty in girls

As with boys, hormones are involved when a girl starts puberty. The main female sex hormone is **estrogen**. It is this hormone that triggers the changes that take place in a girl's body during puberty. These changes include:

- a growth spurt as she gets taller
- a change in body shape, as her breasts develop and fat is laid down on her hips and thighs
- the growth of body hair.

One of the main changes comes when hormones from the brain trigger the ovaries (the main female sex organs) to start producing sex hormones. These hormones come and go in regular, monthly cycles. Each month, eggs mature in the ovaries and at least one is released into a fallopian tube. The **uterus** (womb) prepares for pregnancy by developing a thick, blood-rich lining. If the released egg is not fertilized, the lining of the uterus is shed from the body, and the whole sequence begins again. This monthly cycle is known as menstruation (more commonly referred to as a period) and starts as a young woman becomes sexually mature (see page 13).

THE SCIENCE YOU LEARN:
THE FEMALE REPRODUCTIVE SYSTEM

The female reproductive system is capable of supporting a new life for nearly ten months as a baby develops in the uterus. In every month of a girl's reproductive life, her body prepares for pregnancy. The only time this process stops is when she is actually pregnant, or at the end of her reproductive life. Eventually there are no more eggs left in the ovaries and so the woman is no longer fertile. This is called **menopause**.

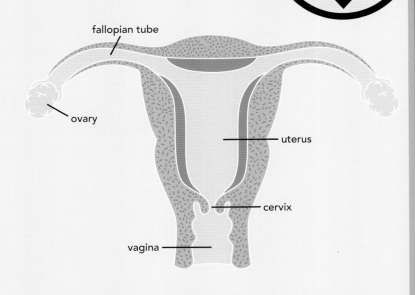

The female reproductive system.

- fallopian tube
- ovary
- uterus
- cervix
- vagina

Weight and fertility risks

The time at which a girl starts her periods is very much related to body mass. Throughout the reproductive life of a woman, regular periods are seen as a sign of fertility. Lowering the body weight and becoming too thin can affect a woman's fertility. Her body will not be getting the nutrients it needs to support a pregnancy and her periods may stop. This kind of weight loss can affect women in less economically developed countries because food is often in short supply.

Female athletes who are training very hard, and women and girls who are affected by the mental illness anorexia nervosa, are also at risk of their periods stopping, making them temporarily infertile. For most women, gaining weight is enough to restore fertility, but sometimes it is lost forever.

If a woman is exceptionally thin, for whatever reason, her periods may stop as her body avoids the demands of pregnancy.

Conception and Pregnancy

As discussed in the previous chapter, after puberty men make sperm all the time. For girls and women the situation is different—eggs mature and are released about once every 28 days. The egg only lives for about 24 hours once it is released. This is the time when a woman can become pregnant—the time when she is fertile.

The journey to conception

The egg has a very gentle journey from the ovary to the uterus. Once a ripe egg bursts out of the mature follicle in the ovary it is gathered into the fallopian tube. It is then carried toward the waiting uterus by many tiny, hair-like cilia. These cilia beat to create currents in the fluid to move the egg along.

Sperm have to work much harder. During sexual intercourse, semen—the nutrient rich liquid containing the sperm—is released high in the vagina, near the cervix. The sperm swim furiously, constantly beating their tails. This, along with **contractions** of the muscles in the female reproductive tract, moves them through the uterus and toward the fallopian tubes.

The moment of conception when a potential new life begins.

Many of the sperm do not make it far enough to cluster around the egg. Every time a man ejaculates, roughly 40 million sperm are released. Only a few thousand of these will reach the egg. Once there, special **enzymes** in the head of each sperm digest the protective layers around the egg. Finally, one sperm penetrates the egg itself. Immediately, chemical reactions take place that make sure no more sperm can get in. The nuclei of the egg and the sperm fuse (join together). This is the moment of conception—a unique new human cell has been formed!

THE SCIENCE YOU LEARN: THE MENSTRUAL CYCLE

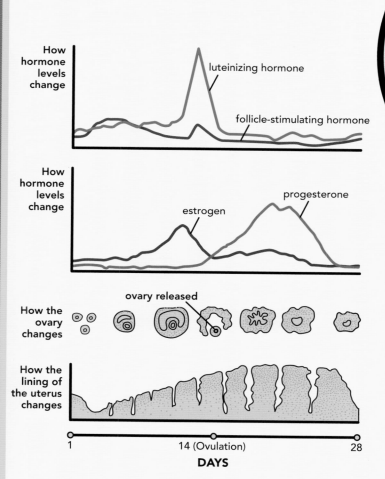

How hormone levels change

luteinizing hormone

follicle-stimulating hormone

How hormone levels change

estrogen

progesterone

ovary released

How the ovary changes

How the lining of the uterus changes

1   14 (Ovulation)   28

DAYS

The menstrual cycle means that women are only fertile for a short time every 28 days. It is usually around day 14 when the mature egg is released from the ovary. However, because sperm can live in a woman's body for some time, having sex up to five days before ovulation can result in the fertilization of an egg and pregnancy.

The menstrual cycle in girls and women is the result of many different hormones working together. These hormones affect the lining of the uterus, the maturing of an egg in the ovary, and the release of the egg at **ovulation**.

Becoming pregnant

If an egg and a sperm meet and fuse, a new cell is formed. This is called a zygote. This zygote rapidly starts to divide as it moves along the fallopian tube toward the uterus. When it reaches the uterus, the zygote has become an early embryo. This is a ball of approximately 50 to 100 cells and is known as a **blastocyst**. At this stage, implantation must take place if the pregnancy is to be successful.

During the first stages of the menstrual cycle the lining of the uterus builds up and thickens, developing a rich blood supply. The early embryo settles, implants itself into this thick lining, and begins to grow into it, taking food and oxygen from the blood vessels. This is the beginning of the formation of the **placenta** (see page 16), and is a sign that pregnancy has truly begun.

Once the embryo has implanted in the uterus, chemical signals are sent. These trigger the production of other hormones in the mother's body and prevent the lining of the uterus from being shed. The woman does not have her usual monthly period. This is the first clue that she might be pregnant.

Symptoms of pregnancy

"I always knew I was pregnant very quickly, even without a pregnancy test. I am a very energetic person, but by the time I was six weeks pregnant I felt very tired indeed. My breasts became tender and, worst of all, I started being sick. I suffered from really bad morning sickness. I didn't just feel nauseous, I was violently sick. It wasn't just in the mornings either—I was sick 30 to 40 times a day, from early morning to late at night. Everything smelled horrible! I lost almost 13 kg [30 pounds] in weight in the first 15 to 20 weeks of each of my pregnancies. However, it didn't put me off and I now have four wonderful children to show for it!"

Ann Fullick, science writer and mother of four sons.

CUTTING EDGE:
PREGNANCY TESTING

Pregnancy tests respond to the changing hormones produced by the body. In the past, pregnancy testing depended on watching the effect of urine from a possibly pregnant woman on female xenopus toads. If the woman was pregnant, the toad laid eggs! These tests were carried out in special labs and the results weren't available for some time.

Modern pregnancy tests can be done at home. They still rely on testing the urine, but modern tests involve special chemicals, known as monoclonal antibodies, not toads. The chemicals respond to low levels of the first hormones made during pregnancy. The woman uses a simple test stick and knows the result within minutes of taking the test. It is possible to get a positive pregnancy test as early as the day a period is due, although the test is more reliable if it is carried out a few days later.

A cross in the square window indicates a positive pregnancy test. Pregnancy can be confirmed as early as on the fourteenth day after conception.

Early pregnancy

A human pregnancy is calculated from the first day of the last period (rather than from the moment of conception) and lasts 40 weeks on average. Probably 60 to 80 percent of all conceptions do not last until the end of pregnancy. Many fail to implant in the uterus and others **miscarry** in the first 8 to 12 weeks. After the first 12 weeks, the chances of survival improve.

The developing fetus relies on its mother for food and oxygen and to get rid of waste products, such as carbon dioxide and urea. This happens in the placenta. The placenta is a unique organ made of tissue from the mother and fetal tissue. In order for it to work properly it is important that the placenta forms correctly and in the right position in the uterus.

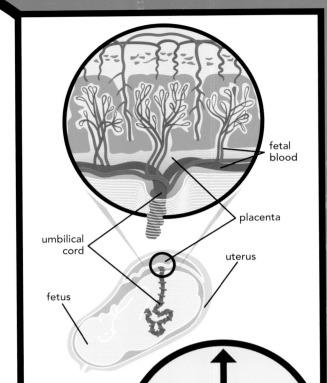

fetal blood

placenta

umbilical cord

uterus

fetus

The placenta provides the growing fetus with everything it needs from the blood of its mother.

Development of the embryo

In the first 12 weeks, the embryo develops from a single cell to a tiny, almost fully formed human being. The cells divide repeatedly, gradually becoming more specialized, until they form tissues (such as muscle) and organs (such as the brain, heart, and the stomach). After eight weeks the embryo looks recognizably human and is known as a fetus.

After fertilization, the cells divide rapidly before implantation.

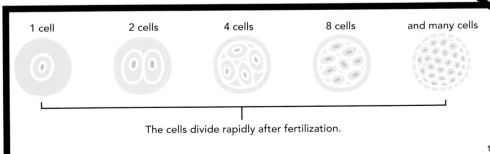

1 cell

2 cells

4 cells

8 cells

and many cells

The cells divide rapidly after fertilization.

About 4 days after fertilization the cells become a blastocyst and can now imbed in the lining of the uterus.

Between 12 and 22 weeks, the fetus continues to grow. It sucks its thumb and its heart beats steadily. The limbs start to twitch and move as muscles and reflex actions develop. Mothers can feel these movements beginning at about 16 weeks. Sensations are faint at first, but later kicks and stretches can be very strong. The outline of tiny feet, elbows, and fists can also sometimes be felt through the wall of the mother's abdomen. At 22 weeks, the baby is about 27 cm (10 in.) long, and weighs about 0.4 kg (1 lb). The lungs, and some of the other organs, are still not fully formed. Babies born at this early stage of pregnancy are on the borderline for survival.

The fully developed fetus gives its mother a very swollen belly. →

↑

The fetus at 22 weeks.

From 22 weeks, the fetus grows quickly, various organ systems mature, and fat starts to form. This fat acts as an energy store in the first few days of life, when the baby is not always good at feeding and the milk supply from the mother may be slow.

The skeleton of an early fetus consists of soft, rubbery cartilage rather than bone. During the final months of pregnancy, real bone forms in many areas, although the process takes years before it is fully complete. In the skull, bony plates form with gaps in between them. This has two vital functions: the skull can be squeezed out of shape during birth, giving the baby a better chance of being delivered safely, and it allows space for the brain to grow rapidly after birth. The bones of the skull don't fuse together completely until a person is at least 16 years old.

Surgery before birth

Detailed blood tests and ultrasound scanning (see page 20) have made it increasingly possible for doctors to diagnose problems in a baby long before it is born. Fetal surgery is a recent development to deal with these problems and involves operating on a developing baby before birth.

Some techniques are widely used and few people question them any more. Blood transfusion is one such technique. In some cases, in which the mother and baby have different blood groups, the mother's body makes **antibodies** against her baby's blood. As a result, the developing baby suffers from severe anemia and can even die. Blood transfusions can be carried out through the umbilical cord, with surgery possible from 18 weeks of pregnancy. This has been carried out successfully for some years now. Other techniques, however, are new and still the subject of debate.

These twins, William and James Endter, survived fetal surgery at the University of California in San Francisco to correct a potentially fatal circulatory problem.

In Florida, Dr. Ruben Quintero has developed a revolutionary keyhole surgical technique to save the lives of identical twins suffering from twin-to-twin transfusion syndrome (TTTS). This occurs due to problems in the blood supply, and results with one twin becoming large and swollen and the other small and shrunken. In 90 percent of severe TTTS cases, both twins die. Dr. Quintero uses keyhole instruments with a laser to seal off the faulty blood vessels that are causing the problem inside the mother's uterus. Success rates are improving all the time.

Fetal surgery is a new and controversial area of science.

Another U.S. surgeon, Dr. Joe Bruner, has developed a completely different form of surgery on unborn babies to try to repair the problems of spina bifida before birth. In spina bifida, part of the bony protection of the spine is missing and the exposed spinal nerves can easily be damaged, leading to paralysis. Normally, doctors operate soon after birth to cover the exposed spinal cord with a protective plate, but often the damage has already been done in the womb and during birth.

Dr. Bruner believes that he can reduce the risk of severe disability by carrying out surgery before birth. At roughly 23 weeks of pregnancy, he cuts into the mother's abdomen and moves her womb out of her body, without completely detaching it. He then opens up the womb to expose the fetus with its malformed spine. He and his team then try to create a layer of tissue to protect the tiny spinal cord, before returning the fetus to the womb and stitching everything back together. This surgery is very risky because it could easily trigger contractions, which would lead to the baby being born **prematurely** and perhaps not surviving.

Dr. Bruner is convinced that his trailblazing surgery has the potential to reduce the disability associated with spina bifida, but not all doctors are convinced. The results have not produced clear evidence either way. So far, the children born after Dr. Bruner's surgery have certainly not been disability free. But who can say what they would have been like without surgery? Some people also feel it is unethical to try out new techniques on unborn babies. What do you think?

Monitoring the baby

A high standard of **prenatal care** for both mother and baby involves:

- advice and education for the mother about various topics, from good nutrition to the importance of breast-feeding
- screening the mother for diseases that might affect her developing baby
- monitoring the mother's blood pressure throughout pregnancy. High blood pressure can put the mother and baby at risk of **pre-eclampsia**
- routine ultrasound scans before 24 weeks of pregnancy, to monitor the growth of the fetus and to identify any abnormalities of the heart, brain, or limbs
- routine measurements of the growth of the uterus by taking measurements of the mother's "bump"
- listening to the heartbeat of the fetus using a heart monitor
- checking the mother's urine for the presence of sugar (an indication of diabetes) and protein (a sign of high blood pressure or infection), all of which can affect the fetus.

CUTTING EDGE: 3D ULTRASOUND SCANS

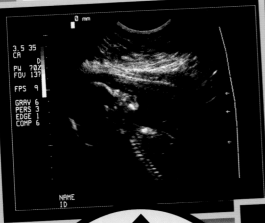

Australian doctors George Kossoff, William Garrett, and David Robinson were the first to publish results on using ultrasound to diagnose fetal abnormalities. In their first successful diagnosis they found kidney abnormalities in a 31-week fetus, allowing doctors to prepare for problems after birth. Now, ultrasound is a vital tool that enables doctors to accurately assess the age of the fetus and check for a number of abnormalities before birth.

Two-dimensional and three-dimensional ultrasound images are an important part of prenatal care.

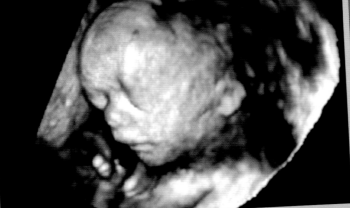

Prenatal care around the world

Good prenatal care does not necessarily require advanced technology, such as ultrasound scans. Health professionals can have a big effect on the health of both mother and baby. They can monitor fetal growth, the mother's blood pressure, and give information about good health care.

In most more economically developed countries, **midwives** and doctors provide prenatal care. Most women benefit from this. However, women in poorer social groups or immigrant populations (where there may be language or culture differences) are less likely to gain access to the best prenatal care.

In many less economically developed countries, family members, friends, and neighbors take care of a pregnant woman. This may work if the pregnancy is normal, but can lead to problems if there are complications.

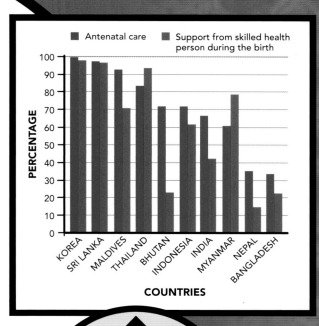

The level of prenatal and health care available in different Asian countries varies considerably.

CASE STUDY

Good prenatal care matters

There seems to be a clear link between good prenatal care and the health of mothers and babies. Recent World Health Organization (WHO) data shows that 70 percent of all deaths from pregnancy and childbirth occurred in just 13 developing countries. Five countries—Bangladesh, India, Indonesia, Myanmar, and Nepal—accounted for 50 percent of these deaths. The chart above shows that these countries have lower percentages of prenatal care and expert support during birth.

Maintaining a Healthy Pregnancy

Almost every aspect of a woman's body is affected by pregnancy. Despite this, most pregnant women throughout the world continue with their normal lives. Of course, they are adapted to do so. If women always became sick or unable to function during pregnancy the human race would have died out long ago!

If the pregnancy is wanted and the woman is healthy, pregnancy can be a very exciting and rewarding time. If the mother is ill, underfed, or if the baby is neither planned nor wanted, it can be a time of great hardship and distress.

Prenatal care (see pages 20–21) involves careful monitoring of the changes in a woman's body during pregnancy to check on her health and the health of the developing fetus.

Changes during pregnancy

One of the most obvious effects of pregnancy is a gain in body mass. The main weight gain takes place from about week 14 to about week 36. Most women gain around 10 kg (22 lbs) but this varies greatly with individuals and different pregnancies. The extra mass should be made up of the baby, placenta, **amniotic fluid**, enlarged uterus and breasts, and extra blood that is formed. Any other weight gain is mainly fat. Health professionals sometimes monitor weight gain to help ensure that the mother doesn't gain too much or too little.

An average woman has about five quarts of blood circulating around her body. During pregnancy, this increases by 30 to 40 percent to supply the extra oxygen and nutrients needed by the developing fetus. Even the heart gets bigger during pregnancy, because it has to work harder and pump more blood. It returns to its normal size within days of the woman giving birth.

Pregnancy around the world

Attitudes toward pregnancy vary greatly in different cultures. In many parts of the world, women continue with hard physical work until they go into **labor**. In countries like the United States and United Kingdom, women often take better care of themselves than usual while pregnant. In biological terms, a normal pregnancy is very stable and a woman can run, ride horses and bicycles, do heavy work, and even take a normal fall without any real risk to the baby. The biggest problem is if the woman hurts herself—for example, by falling off a horse—since this could put the baby at risk.

Keeping healthy and active means mother and baby are more likely to reach the end of the pregnancy in good health.

Some aspects of modern life are not ideal for pregnant women. Sitting for long periods of time (in front of a computer, for example) can lead to blood pooling in the pelvis, and standing for too long can result in blood pooling in the legs. In both of these cases the blood supply to the developing baby may be reduced. Ideally, pregnant women should exercise regularly to keep their circulation going and to help ensure they are healthy as they approach the time of delivery.

Keeping the fetus safe

The body systems of women have evolved to keep a developing fetus safe in the uterus. As it grows to full term, the fetus is protected by the mother's body and by the cushioning amniotic fluid. But it cannot be protected from every danger.

During the first 12 weeks of pregnancy, the major organ systems of an embryo are being formed and the embryo is most vulnerable to any chemicals that may be taken into the mother's body. For this reason, all women must be very careful about what they put into their bodies while they are pregnant. However, many women do not realize they are pregnant for many weeks, maybe because they have irregular periods or have not been trying to get pregnant. This means that sometimes women take chemicals into their body without realizing an embryo is at risk.

Food...

Food eaten by the mother can affect the health of the fetus. Certain minerals and vitamins are vital for the developing baby to form and grow properly. For example, spina bifida is a condition in which some of the vertebrae do not form properly in early pregnancy. The main spinal nerve is exposed and may be damaged. The tendency to have children with spina bifida can run in families, so it cannot be completely prevented. However, scientists and doctors have shown that low levels of folic acid, one of the B vitamins, is linked to the condition as well. If women take a folic acid supplement before they get pregnant, and for the first three months of pregnancy, the risk of spina bifida can be reduced by up to 70 percent.

Some of the organisms that cause food poisoning in adults can also cause problems in unborn babies. For example, the bacteria *Listeria monocytogenes* can be found in unpasteurized cheeses, unwashed vegetables, and raw meats. It doesn't cause serious problems for adults. However, a woman infected by this bacteria early on in pregnancy will probably have a miscarriage, while later in pregnancy her baby may be permanently damaged or die soon after birth.

This premature baby was born with Fetal Alcohol Syndrome. This is a condition that would never be seen if all women avoided alcoholic drinks when they are pregnant.

...and drink!

When a pregnant woman drinks alcohol it passes easily across the placenta into the blood of her developing fetus. An adult's liver can break down moderate amounts of alcohol easily, but a fetus cannot. If a woman drinks regularly, her fetus may develop Fetal Alcohol Syndrome. Depending on which stage of pregnancy a fetus is exposed to alcohol, it is likely to be born early and have a low birth weight. Babies that have been exposed to alcohol often have facial abnormalities, heart defects, and may have brain problems that cause sight and hearing difficulties, seizures, and poor coordination. Doctors are not sure if there is a safe alcohol consumption limit during pregnancy. The damage can be done in the very early stages of pregnancy, so most doctors and governments advise women to avoid alcohol completely if trying to conceive and when pregnant.

Legal drugs (medicines)

Doctors prescribe medicines to make us better. However, some of those medicines can cause terrible damage to a developing fetus. Great care is taken by doctors to make sure that pregnant women and their babies are not put at risk, because there have been some tragedies in the past.

The thalidomide tragedy

Thalidomide is a medicine that was developed in the 1950s as a sleeping pill. Doctors found it also relieved morning sickness and prescribed it to many pregnant women. Thalidomide is very safe for adults, but when given to women in early pregnancy it prevents their fetus from developing limbs normally. Thousands of babies were born with severe limb deformities before doctors and scientists realized that thalidomide was the cause. As a result of this tragedy, all new medicines now have to be tested on animals to see if they affect developing fetuses.

Many of the people affected by thalidomide are living full and active lives in spite of the limb deformities caused by the drug.

Illegal drugs

When people are addicted to illegal drugs, they are in a situation that can badly affect their health. If a woman is using illegal drugs when she is pregnant, she is forcing that choice on her unborn child. Many illegal drugs can damage a developing fetus. For example, heroin use is linked to an increased risk of miscarriages, premature births, and stillbirths (when a baby is born dead). Another terrible side effect of a mother using drugs is that the fetus will also become addicted. Once the baby is born, and the supply of the drug is cut off, it suffers all the symptoms of drug withdrawal that any adult addict would face. This is not a good start in life and can prove fatal.

Smoking

When a pregnant woman smokes, nicotine (a drug found in cigarettes) passes through the placenta into the blood of her baby. The unborn baby then becomes a nicotine addict. After smoking a cigarette, up to 10 percent of the mother's blood is filled with the poisonous gas **carbon monoxide**, instead of oxygen. As a result of smoking, the fetus may suffer from a lack of oxygen. This can lead to growth problems, reduced development of the brain, and even a premature birth. Babies born to smokers are more likely to be stillborn, or to die in the first few days after birth, than the babies of nonsmokers. Giving up smoking—or better still, never smoking at all—greatly increases the chances of having a healthy baby.

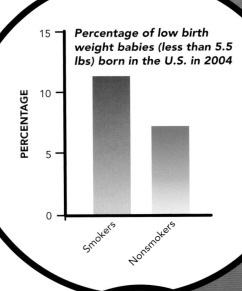

Percentage of low birth weight babies (less than 5.5 lbs) born in the U.S. in 2004

Smoking increases the risk of a premature birth. Babies that are born too early are more likely to have health problems or die.

Genetic Inheritance

Most families have characteristics that are passed down from one generation to the next. People often find it interesting when one family member looks very much like another. All of your characteristics—the shape of your nose, if you have dimples, the color of your eyes, hair, and skin—are inherited (they have been passed on to you from your parents).

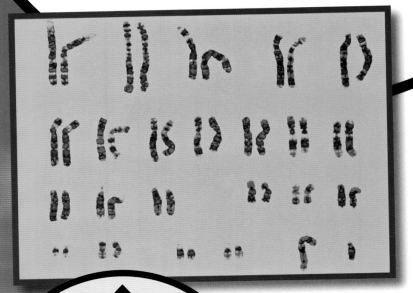

A complete set of human chromosomes. These come from a male. They contain all the information needed to make and organize new cells. What is more, they contain the blueprint for a whole new human being!

How genetics works

The resemblance you have to your parents is the result of **genetic information** passed on in the gametes (egg and sperm) from which you developed. This genetic information is carried in the nucleus of your cells. Within the nucleus there are thread-like structures called chromosomes. These chromosomes are made of a special chemical called **DNA (deoxyribonucleic acid)**. This is where the genetic information is actually stored.

DNA is a long molecule made up of two strands that are twisted together to make a spiral. This is known as a double helix (imagine it as a rope ladder that has been twisted).

Each different type of living organism in species that reproduce sexually has a characteristic number of chromosomes in its body cells. Humans have 46, while turkeys have 82! Half of your chromosomes come from your mother and half from your father, so you have 23 pairs of chromosomes in your normal body cells.

Each of the chromosomes contains thousands of **genes**, joined together. The genes are your units of inheritance. Each gene is a small section of the long DNA molecule and affects a different characteristic about you. Both of the chromosomes in a pair carry genes that control the same things in the same place in your body. Some of your characteristics are decided by a single pair of genes, such as whether your thumb is straight or curved, and whether you have dimples when you smile. However, most of your characteristics—for example, your hair and eye color—are the result of several different genes working together.

If one parent has dimples, there is a good chance that they will produce a child with dimples.

THE SCIENCE YOU LEARN:
THE INHERITANCE OF DOMINANT AND RECESSIVE ALLELES

Each gene has at least two different forms. Each form is known as an **allele**. For example, the gene for the shape of your thumb has two alleles, for straight and curved. Some alleles can control the development of a characteristic even when they are only present on one of your chromosomes. These alleles are dominant, and examples include the alleles for dimples and dangly earlobes. Others only control the development of a characteristic if they are present on both chromosomes (in other words, no dominant allele is present). These alleles are recessive, and examples include the alleles for no dimples and attached earlobes.

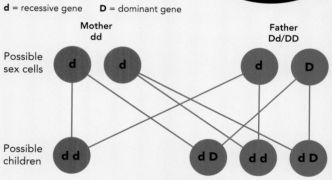

d = recessive gene   **D** = dominant gene

Mother
dd

Father
Dd/DD

Possible sex cells

Possible children

50% chance of dimples
50% chance of no dimples

Genetic crosses like these can be used to show the chance a child has of inheriting a specific set of alleles.

Mutations

Mutations are tiny changes in the long strands of DNA. Many occur through mistakes made in copying the DNA when cells divide. Others occur as a result of certain chemicals (mutagenic chemicals) or from exposure to ionizing radiation. Many mutations have no effect on the characteristics of an organism and some mutations are useful. Occasionally, mutations are harmful and can cause **genetic diseases**, affecting the way a baby develops in the uterus.

Genetic diseases

Some genetic diseases, such as cystic fibrosis, are caused by the mutation of a single gene. Others, such as Down's syndrome, are the result of whole chromosome problems. Some have a devastating effect on the body and can be fatal. Others cause relatively minor problems which can now be dealt with.

CASE STUDY

A modern dilemma

It is now possible to check embryos even before they implant in the uterus. In this case, eggs harvested from the mother are fertilized with sperm from the father in a laboratory. The genetic makeup of these early embryos is then checked and only healthy ones are returned to the mother's womb. It may be possible in the future to change the genetic makeup of the embryos using genetic engineering. This could ensure that the embryos are free of all genetic diseases. However, this raises many ethical questions including what level of interference is acceptable to ensure a healthy baby?

People affected by cystic fibrosis need to take lots of medicine and undergo daily physical therapy. But this does not keep them from making the most of life!

Testing for genetic diseases

Some people have a higher risk than average of having a child that is affected by a genetic disease. For example, older women have an increased risk of giving birth to a child with Down's syndrome. There are ways to test for such diseases (two are outlined below), but they can raise some difficult ethical issues.

- Amniocentesis is a prenatal test that involves taking a small sample of the fluid from around the developing fetus at about 16 weeks of pregnancy. Fetal cells are then grown and tested for a variety of chromosome abnormalities.
- Chorionic villus testing can be carried out earlier in the pregnancy (at roughly 12 weeks), and involves taking a small sample of tissue from the developing placenta and examining it.

Both of these tests involve a risk of miscarriage, regardless of whether the fetus is healthy or not. If parents get a positive result (a genetic disease does exist), they then have to decide whether to continue with the pregnancy or **terminate** it. Both choices raise ethical issues. Is it right to end a pregnancy because the fetus has a serious genetic disease? Is it right to knowingly bring a child with a severe genetic condition into the world? These are questions that science alone cannot answer.

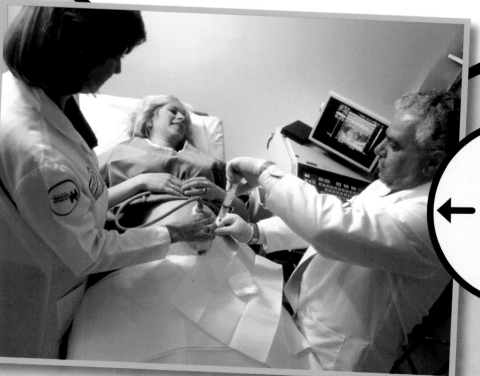

This woman is having amniocentesis. The process carries some risk to the fetus.

Giving Birth

By the end of pregnancy, the fetus is outgrowing the uterus and the placenta is less efficient at providing everything the fetus needs. At this stage the fetus is ready to leave its mother's body.

A normal delivery

The fetus triggers the birth process, known as labor. Special chemicals are produced which make the muscles of the uterus contract. There are three main stages in the birth process:

- During the first stage, the contractions of the uterus gradually get closer together and stronger. The goal of these contractions is to dilate (open up) the cervix, from a gap of 2 to 10 cm (0.1 to 4 in.). This needs to happen in order to allow the head of the baby to move through.
- The second stage of labor begins once the cervix is fully dilated. At this point, the baby can be delivered. The muscles of the uterus and the abdomen work together to push the baby out of the uterus, through the cervix, and along the vagina.
- Once the baby is born, the placenta peels away from the wall of the uterus. The blood vessels that have been supplying blood to the fetus close down. During this third stage, the muscles of the uterus push the placenta out of the body. Sometimes women are given an injection to help the body release the placenta as quickly as possible.

The short distance from the mother's uterus to the outside world is a dangerous journey.

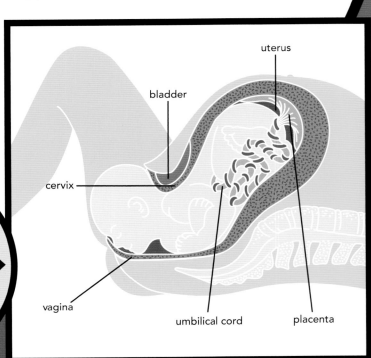

uterus

bladder

cervix

vagina

umbilical cord

placenta

Pain relief

The average time for a first labor is 8–12 hours, but it can vary from minutes to days. The pain experienced by women during labor also varies greatly. In most economically developed countries, hospitals can provide effective ways of helping women manage the pain. These include breathing and relaxation exercises, inhaling "gas and air" (a mixture of nitrous oxide and oxygen that eases the pain), injecting meperidine (a drug, commonly known by the brand name Demerol, that gives effective pain relief), and administering an epidural or spinal anesthetic (anesthetic injected into the fluid around the spinal nerve to block pain sensations).

Cesarean sections

Sometimes it isn't possible for a baby to be born naturally. The baby may be very large, the gap in the pelvis very small, or the muscles of the uterus unable to contract strongly enough. If the fetus starts to become distressed, or if the doctors feel there is a physical or medical reason why a woman might struggle to give birth naturally, the baby can be removed from the uterus during an operation known as a **Cesarean**. These are now usually performed with a spinal anesthetic. This means that the mother is awake when the baby is born and her partner can be there.

↑ A successful delivery is a cause for happiness and celebration. Yet each year about half a million women die of pregnancy and birth complications. Many of these deaths could be avoided.

The changes at birth

The transformation from a fetus in the uterus to a baby that breathes and feeds independently is a huge one. Some of the changes a fetus goes through are:

- During delivery, the bones of the skull can overlap to allow the head to pass through the mother's pelvis. After birth, the bones spread out, although the baby may have a rather odd-shaped head for a few days after delivery!
- As the baby draws its first breath, the lungs need to inflate. This is dependent on **lung surfactant**.
- Most of the fetus' blood bypasses the lungs along an extra blood vessel. Once the baby is born, this blood vessel has to close off so the blood goes to the lungs to pick up oxygen. Also, in the fetus, the right and left hand sides of the heart are connected by a hole through the center. After birth, this hole has to close so the two sides of the heart become completely separate. This keeps the oxygenated blood in the lungs from mixing with the deoxygenated blood collected in the body.
- The liver has to work much harder after birth, because the baby can no longer rely on the mother's body systems to deal with, clean, and monitor the blood.

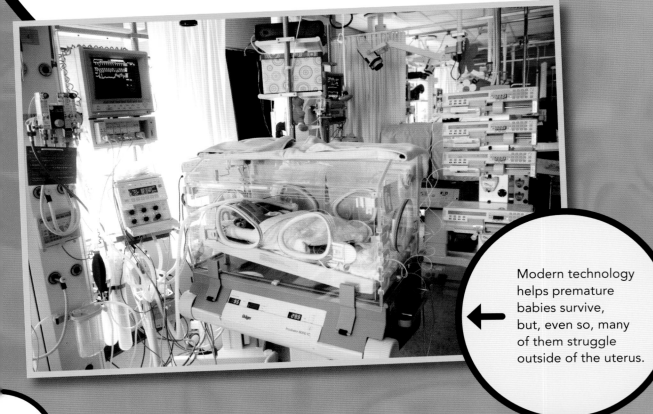

Modern technology helps premature babies survive, but, even so, many of them struggle outside of the uterus.

Born too soon

A normal human pregnancy lasts for roughly 40 weeks. However, sometimes a baby is born too soon. Anything earlier than 37 weeks is known as a premature (or preterm) birth. The time the baby has spent developing in the uterus is the single most important factor that will decide whether it lives or dies. For example, if the baby is at about 28 weeks when it is born, a single extra day of development can influence its chances of survival by up to 3 percent.

Babies born between 23 and 26 weeks may weigh less than 0.5 kg (1 lb) and struggle to survive. Such babies are usually placed in an incubator, which breathes for them and keeps them warm, and they are fed through a tube into their veins or stomach. The idea is to mimic the uterus in every way possible.

If born between 26 and 32 weeks, the chances of survival improve, but there may still be many problems. By 32 to 34 weeks, the lungs of the baby mature and it can begin to breathe unaided. After 34 weeks, the outlook for most babies is very good and they will often survive unharmed by their early arrival into the world.

Worth the risk?

The treatment of the most premature babies raises a number of ethical issues. It is expensive and time consuming to keep a very premature baby alive, and many die despite the treatment. The majority of those that survive have some degree of disability. The most severely affected need expensive treatment throughout their lives. Is this a good use of limited funding? And is it fair to keep a baby alive when it has a high chance of being disabled? In some countries, babies born before 23 weeks are not given intensive resuscitation. In other countries, all live births are given the same chance. What do you think?

Fertility Problems

Most people assume they will get pregnant easily, but as many as one couple in six do not succeed. Even young, fertile couples may not **conceive** right away. As people get older, their fertility naturally falls away. Lifestyle choices, such as smoking, drinking, and being underweight or overweight also reduce fertility levels.

For some couples, the problems are more complex. In about one-third of infertility cases there is a problem in the way the woman's reproductive system is working. In another third, the problem lies in the man's reproductive system. In another third, both the man and the woman are less fertile than normal and the combination causes problems. In some cases, there is no apparent reason why the couple don't get pregnant. This is very puzzling for doctors and extremely difficult for the couple.

A blocked fallopian tube can be seen in the top right of this hysterosalpingogram X-ray. The orange area is the uterus.

Infertility in women

If a woman does not ovulate, she cannot get pregnant. This is because there is no egg to fertilize. Some women do not ovulate because they have no eggs in their ovaries. The only way they can become pregnant is if another woman donates some of her eggs. Many women who do not ovulate do actually have eggs, but problems with the hormones that cause the follicles to ripen in the ovaries and release the eggs means they do not ovulate. This can be overcome with artificial hormones, known as **fertility drugs**. However, the dose has to be carefully managed and the response closely monitored to prevent multiple pregnancies—when the mother carries more than one baby (see page 42).

THE SCIENCE YOU LEARN:
THE JOURNEY OF THE FERTILIZED EGG

When an egg leaves the ovary it moves along the fallopian tube on currents of fluid, wafted along by cilia, which line the tube. Fertilization of the egg by the sperm takes place in the fallopian tube. The early embryo then continues along the tube until it reaches the uterus.

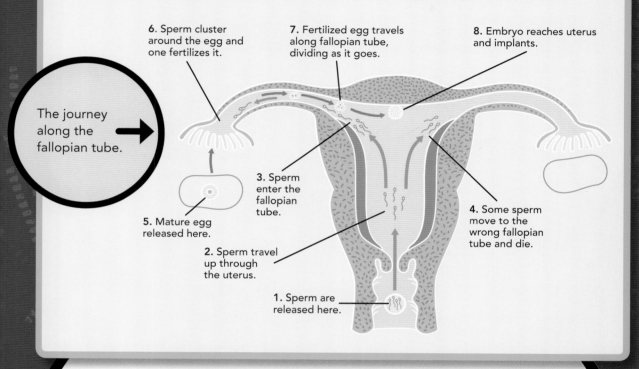

6. Sperm cluster around the egg and one fertilizes it.

7. Fertilized egg travels along fallopian tube, dividing as it goes.

8. Embryo reaches uterus and implants.

The journey along the fallopian tube.

5. Mature egg released here.

3. Sperm enter the fallopian tube.

4. Some sperm move to the wrong fallopian tube and die.

2. Sperm travel up through the uterus.

1. Sperm are released here.

Sometimes the problem is anatomical (to do with the person's bodily structure). The fallopian tubes, which lead from the ovaries to the uterus, may be twisted, scarred, or blocked. This may mean the sperm cannot get through to meet the egg or, more commonly, the fertilized egg cannot move through to implant in the uterus. Sometimes this problem can be solved by surgery, but often other solutions are required.

One common cause of blocked or scarred tubes is sexually transmitted diseases (STD). A number of different sexually transmitted diseases, such as gonorrhea and chlamydia, are very difficult to detect in their early stages, particularly in women. If left untreated, they can cause inflammation and scarring in the fallopian tubes, so the woman does not find out she is infertile until she wants to start a family. This is one of several good reasons for taking care of your sexual health.

Male infertility

However regularly a woman ovulates, she will not get pregnant if her partner is not producing plenty of fertile sperm. Normal, healthy semen contains at least 20 million sperm per 1 cm³ (0.06 in.³) of semen (that's only about 1/5 of a teaspoon of semen). Once the sperm count falls below this it starts to affect fertility levels. Only about one sperm in every 2,000 makes the journey from the cervix to the fallopian tubes—the lower the sperm count, the lower the chance of conceiving.

Sperm need to be active and swim strongly. Also, every man produces some abnormal sperm with two heads or tails instead of one, or with broken necks. If the proportion of abnormal sperm is too high, fertility levels are affected because abnormal sperm do not fertilize the egg.

In the past, the only solution to male infertility was to use donated sperm from another man. As infertility treatment has developed, scientists and doctors have found new ways of helping infertile men become fathers.

Using techniques like this, a single sperm can be injected into an egg to overcome male fertility problems.

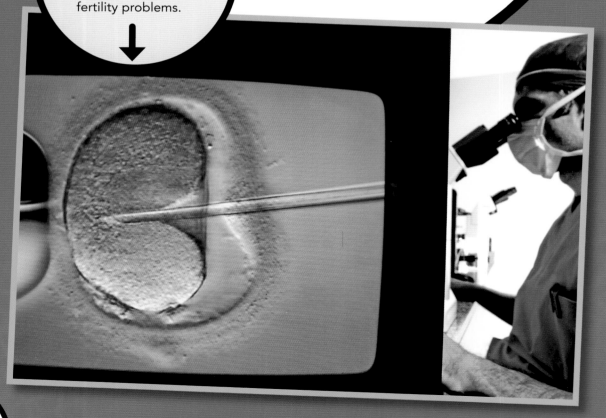

38

IVF and other infertility treatments

If lifestyle changes and fertility treatments have not worked, more sophisticated methods can be used. The best known of these is **in vitro fertilization** (IVF). This involves removing eggs from a woman and fertilizing them with sperm outside her body. The fertilized eggs are then allowed to grow for up to five days into early embryos. Between one and three of the healthiest embryos are inserted back inside the uterus, in the middle (the best place for implantation to take place). Clinics are working toward inserting a single embryo, to reduce the risk of multiple pregnancies, but sometimes two or three are inserted to increase the chances of success.

This procedure sounds simple, but involves considerable intervention by doctors. Fertility drugs are used to stimulate the ovaries to produce many ripe eggs, and the uterus is then prepared for pregnancy using other artificial hormones. Harvesting, fertilizing, and returning the embryos uses ultrasound scans, microscopes, and other technology. Once an embryo has implanted in the uterus, the pregnancy should continue to develop as normal.

1. Fertility drugs cause many eggs to ripen at the same time.

2. The eggs are collected and placed in a special solution in a petri dish.

4. The eggs and sperm are mixed.

3. A sample of semen is collected.

5. The eggs are checked to make sure that they have been fertilized and are growing well.

6. When the fertilized eggs have divided to form tiny balls of cells, they are placed in the mother's uterus.

IVF is an expensive and complex procedure that carries no guarantee of success.

CUTTING EDGE: DIFFICULT DECISIONS

Many variations of IVF have been developed to help with different types of infertility. For example, doctors can inject a single sperm into an egg (this is known as Intra Cytoplasmic Sperm Injection, or ICSI). This has revolutionized treatment for infertile men. As long as one single live sperm can be found—or even an immature sperm collected from the testes—it can be used to fertilize an egg. ICSI has even made it possible for people with genetic diseases, which usually result in infertility (such as cystic fibrosis), to father their own children. This makes the affected individuals very happy, but means the baby will almost certainly carry the gene for the genetic illness. There are people who claim this is not an ethical use of science. What do you think?

Ethical Issues Surrounding IVF

New reproductive technologies raise many different ethical issues and are the source of much debate.

The success rate of treatment

Many different factors can affect the success of IVF. The table below shows the effect age has on the success rates of IVF treatment in women. Victoria Wright, the author of a similar U.S. report, says figures like these are *"a reminder that age remains a primary factor with respect to pregnancy success, and younger women have greater success than older women, even with technology."*

Another factor is that the success rate when using frozen eggs or embryos is much lower. When fresh eggs (that have been donated by younger women) are used, the success rate is roughly 50 percent, almost regardless of the age of the mother.

Some IVF clinics will only deal with younger couples, or with couples who have not already had several failed attempts. These clinics are therefore likely to have higher success rates than clinics that deal with more difficult cases—but it does not necessarily mean they are better at the job!

IVF success rates following treatment carried out in 2003 and 2004 in the United Kingdom, as published in the 2006–7 *HFEA Guide to Infertility*.

Age of woman	% of successful pregnancies per cycle using fresh eggs
Under 35	28.2
35–37	23.6
38–39	18.3
40–42	10.6
42+	Not given

Freezing sperm, eggs, and embryos

Frozen sperm has been used in infertility treatment for many years. More recently, excess human embryos produced during IVF have been frozen, then thawed, and implanted into their mother's uterus at a later date. The embryos seem unharmed and appear to develop normally. However, there is continued debate surrounding problems caused when a couple separates while embryos are in storage. If this happens, who owns them?

Sometimes embryos are stored for a woman who is to undergo cancer treatment that will make her infertile. However, a recent European Court of Human Rights ruling upheld a man's right to not become a father, even though it denied a woman her only chance of carrying her own biological children. New developments mean that human eggs can now be stored before they are fertilized—but the chances of success with frozen eggs are much less than with fresh ones.

Without IVF, none of these people would have been born!

Selecting embryos

The genetic makeup of early embryos can now be examined and checked. People with serious genetic diseases can be sure that only embryos free from the disease are selected and implanted into the mother. However, some people think it is unethical to select embryos in this way. They believe that life begins at conception and so destroying an embryo made up of a few cells is like killing a child.

With the development of **genetic modification**, in the future embryos could be changed to remove genetic diseases before they are implanted. Some people fear that embryos might be manipulated to give them desirable features (such as higher levels of intelligence or good looks), rather than to avoid disease. This could lead to "designer babies"—made to order with specific characteristics specified by the couple—and an underclass of people who cannot afford genetic manipulation.

Multiple births

Even with natural conception, twins, triplets, and even quadruplets are sometimes born. More than one egg may be released and fertilized, resulting in siblings who share a uterus at the same time. Sometimes a fertilized egg divides and separates once or more, resulting in a multiple birth in which all the babies share the same genetic material because they came from the same fertilized egg (see box below).

Multiple pregnancies—even twins—increase the risks for both mother and babies by up to six times. It puts greater strain on the body of the mother to support more than one fetus as it grows. There are more risks for the babies as well, especially if they are identical and share a placenta. One twin may take more of the resources than the other, which may result in the death of the other twin. The delivery can be more difficult, with one baby having to get in line and wait to be born. The second baby may suffer from a lack of oxygen at this stage. Babies that result from multiple pregnancies are almost always smaller than normal singletons (single babies), so the newborn infants are at greater risk of breathing problems and even death. Multiple pregnancies are monitored very carefully to try to prevent problems.

THE SCIENCE YOU LEARN: IDENTICAL AND FRATERNAL TWINS

There are two types of twin pregnancies. One results in the birth of identical twins. This occurs when one egg is fertilized by one sperm, then almost immediately the zygote formed splits in two. Each of these will develop into a separate baby with the exact same genetic information. Identical twins are, therefore, always the same gender. The other type of twin pregnancy results in the birth of fraternal twins. This occurs when two eggs are released at the same time (multiple ovulation) and are fertilized by different sperm. Each baby will have its own unique genetic code. Fraternal twins will not look identical and can be different sexes.

Big multiple births

The biggest risk with using fertility drugs is that far too many eggs will be released at once, resulting in large, multiple births. This was more of a problem in the early days of the treatment and doctors are very careful about the dosage they use, but some women react unexpectedly strongly to the drugs.

Sometimes multiple births do well—but more often they result in tragedy. The more fetuses that are implanted, the bigger the risk. Six babies born at the same time (sextuplets) occasionally survive. The Walton sextuplets—all girls—were born in the United Kingdom in 1983 and are now young adults. In 2002, the Harris family in the United States gave birth to the world's first African-American sextuplets. The four boys and two girls continue to do well. Such cases are few and it is rare for all babies of sextuplets to survive when they are born. Often, all the babies die.

In rare cases as many as eight babies (octuplets) are conceived and born. So far there is not one case of all eight babies surviving. The Chukwu octuplets, born in 1998 in the United States, have the best survival rate recorded—seven of the eight children are still alive and doing well.

When large multiple pregnancies are diagnosed, couples are now offered the opportunity of pregnancy reduction. This reduces the number of fetuses to give the remaining babies the best possible chance of survival. Many people take this option, but for moral and ethical reasons some do not. All of the babies will often then die.

The birth of all surviving sextuplets is very rare, so there is a lot of media interest. The Walton sextuplets are now in their twenties, but people still want to know how they are doing.

Taking Care of the Baby

When a human baby is born it will not survive for long without adult care. Newborn babies need food; they cannot control their own body temperature very well, so they need to be kept warm; and they need physical contact and interaction with people who care for them. In most societies around the world this comes from the parents and the extended family.

The responses of newborn babies are small and subtle—they do not have very good control over their muscles. But if parents watch for those responses and react to them, the bond between them will develop as fast as possible. The baby is more likely to be calm and content as a result. For example, when a baby is born it already responds to the voices it recognizes from hearing them when it was in the uterus. When it hears a familiar voice, it will look toward the source of the sound and may calm down if crying. The voice of the mother gets the strongest response, but the sound of the father, and even brothers and sisters, are also often recognized.

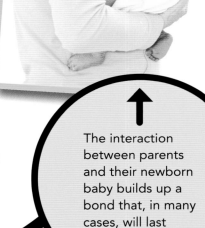

The interaction between parents and their newborn baby builds up a bond that, in many cases, will last throughout life.

Holding close

In most societies around the world, a newborn baby remains in close contact with its mother all the time. It sleeps with her, is carried around on her back or front throughout the day, and is fed by her on demand. Babies need physical contact and comfort, they need to be warm, and they need to be fed. When these needs are met, babies are mostly content and happy, and they grow and thrive.

Interestingly, it is more often only in the more economically developed countries that babies are routinely deprived of the contact they crave. Here babies are usually kept in cribs, bassinets, and strollers. Women in these countries often take pride in returning to work a very short time after their baby is born, and in many cases leaving the baby in the care of day care providers or nannies. While no one doubts that children in these countries have plenty of food, stimulation, and love, it may be that in some ways they are deprived of the almost constant human contact that babies in some other cultures enjoy.

CASE STUDY

Normal behavior and infant care

In the 1950s and 1960s, U.S. psychologist Harry Harlow carried out some now famous work on baby monkeys. At the time, people thought that children bonded to their mothers because their mothers fed them. Harlow's work involved taking baby rhesus monkeys from their mothers and putting them in cages. In each cage were two artificial "mothers." One was made of wire and provided a bottle of milk. The other "mother" had no milk, but was covered in warm, cuddly material. The babies spent as little time as possible with the wire mother, only visiting her to feed. They spent most of their time with the cuddly mother. Harlow's results suggested that cuddling and contact were very important for normal development. He also showed, in other experiments, that to develop and behave normally young monkeys needed their real mothers—but they also needed other monkeys to play and interact with.

The work Harry Harlow carried out with his rhesus monkeys showed that interaction with many different monkeys was important for normal behavior to develop. This also shed light on our understanding of how human parents and babies interact.

Feeding the baby

A mother's body makes the ideal food for human babies. The mammary glands, or breasts, produce milk that has the correct balance of water, protein, fats, sugars, minerals, and vitamins for a human baby.

The composition of a mother's milk changes as the baby grows. The very first milk is known as **colostrum**. This is rich in protein, to stimulate growth, and carbohydrates, an easily digested source of energy. Most importantly, it is full of antibodies. These give the baby immunity from a wide range of diseases, until its own immune system has had a chance to develop. A mother's milk also changes with the weather! In hot weather, it is more dilute to give the baby more fluid. It is sterile and delivered at just the right temperature.

Breast milk is the ideal food for a baby.

Breast-feeding can make loss of excess weight easier after childbirth, since milk production uses calories. Women who are breast-feeding are also less likely to begin ovulating again, so it helps to space out the birth of children. Breast milk is the best food for human babies. The main exception is when the mother is infected with HIV/AIDS, since the virus could be passed on to her baby through her milk.

Understanding formula

In more economically developed countries, many babies are fed with formula. This is usually modified cow's milk that is dried, mixed with boiled water, and fed to a baby through a bottle. There are many reasons for using formula. The mother may be unable to breast-feed, or may find it difficult; she may also want to return to work, from choice or through necessity. Using formula can make feeding easier: it is more filling than human milk, so babies tend to need feeding less often, and using a bottle means other people can feed the baby. However, the balance of food in formula milk is not as well adjusted for the baby, so bottle-fed babies are more likely to become overweight. More importantly, formula contains no antibodies and does not provide protection against disease.

In less economically developed countries, most women breast-feed. However, some companies promote formula in these countries and this can cause problems. Some mothers want to bottle-feed, but cannot afford to buy enough formula, so they underfeed their babies. Also, the water used to make the formula is not always clean and the bottles are often not sterilized. Save the Children (an international charity) reports that an estimated 3,800 children die every day, worldwide, as a result of formula feeding.

Healthy babies, healthy world

Reproduction is an amazing process. The egg and sperm must meet at the right time and then an entire human being develops from that single cell! The developed fetus must make the difficult journey from the uterus to the outside world. As it emerges, great changes have to take place for the baby to live an independent life.

The birth of a baby is an everyday miracle. As you have seen in this book, the work of doctors and scientists has helped us to understand the process better, and to make it safer for both mothers and babies.

This graph shows the results taken from a study done in Brazil, South America. It shows the effects formula feeding has on the risk of a baby dying from diarrhea.

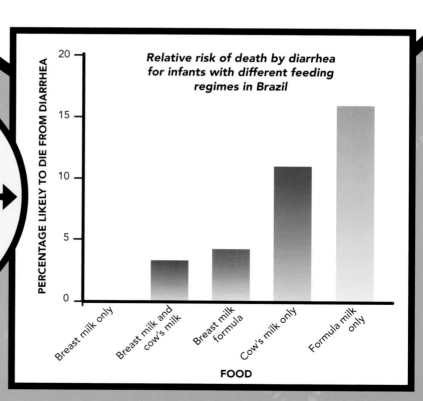

Relative risk of death by diarrhea for infants with different feeding regimes in Brazil

PERCENTAGE LIKELY TO DIE FROM DIARRHEA

FOOD

- Breast milk only
- Breast milk and cow's milk
- Breast milk formula
- Cow's milk only
- Formula milk only

Facts and Figures

The timeline below shows the sequence of events leading from a fertilized egg to a human baby.

Day 0   First day of menstrual period

Day 14   Fertile egg is released from the ovary and fertilized by a healthy sperm

Day 19   Blastocyst reaches the uterus

Day 29   Typically when the woman realizes she has missed her period—pregnancy test may show positive

Day 35   Pregnancy is well established—home pregnancy test will give a positive result

Day 42 (6 weeks)   Embryo is about the size of a small bean: it has a beating heart, tiny limb buds appear, and the stomach and breathing system begin to develop

7 weeks   Embryo has tiny arms and legs, although fingers and toes are webbed; face begins to develop; embryo makes movements as its muscles begin to grow. The mother must be careful—taking certain drugs could damage the developing embryo at this stage.

8 weeks   Embryo roughly 2 cm (0.8 in.) long; mother probably feeling tired, with tender breasts; hormones of early pregnancy may make woman feel nauseous or sick. From this point on, embryo referred to as a fetus.

10 weeks   All major organs in place; embryo is making its own blood cells using its liver. Blood tests can be carried out to check risk level for some genetic diseases. Medical staff should make sure the mother has enough iron in her blood—if not, she will be given iron supplements. Morning sickness and tiredness may be at their worst at this stage.

12 weeks   Fetus roughly the length of an adult thumb; it twitches and moves as a result of muscle reflexes, though it is unlikely the mother can feel these; hands and feet are formed, with minute fingernails and toenails. Many women start to attend regular prenatal visits and make arrangements for where and how the baby will be born. Chorionic villus sampling test will be carried out if needed (because of age of the mother or results of blood tests).

10–14 weeks	Ultrasound scan often carried out; at this stage doctors can get a fairly accurate idea of the age of the fetus by taking careful measurements. Scan also allows medical staff to observe multiple pregnancies.
16 weeks	Fetus getting bigger and more active. Some mothers feel tiny fluttering movements as the fetus kicks and moves very vigorously. Amniocentesis may be offered if there is concern about the possibility of serious genetic problems in the developing fetus.
20 weeks	Pregnancy is showing by now; most mothers can feel baby moving; many people have second ultrasound scan at 18–23 weeks to make sure the fetus is growing normally; often possible to find out gender of baby at this stage
22 weeks	Earliest stage at which baby has chance of surviving a premature birth—almost all babies born this early will die or be severely disabled if they survive
24 weeks	Many organ systems are getting close to maturity; tiny air sacs in lungs begin to produce lung surfactant—once this is in place the baby will be able to breathe if it is born, greatly increasing its chances of a healthy survival. Almost 80 percent of babies born at this stage of pregnancy survive if given intensive high-technology care, although at least 25 percent of survivors will have long-term problems.
28 weeks	Fetus acquires fat ready to survive outside uterus; eyelashes form; organ systems continue to grow and mature; teeth form under gums; babies can hear sounds and respond to light movements on the mother's belly.
32 weeks	Fetus getting bigger and stronger; muscle bulk builds up; it is harder for the fetus to move freely due to lack of space.
36 weeks	Fetus almost ready to be born. Majority of babies settle so that they are head down in their mother's pelvis by this stage—they cannot change again because there isn't room. Head first is the ideal way for a baby to be born—bottom or feet first can be dangerous and in most cases results in doctors performing a Cesarean. From now on, the baby may be born and has a very high chance of being delivered safely.
40 weeks	Baby is fully formed and ready to be born; placenta gradually becomes less efficient; space very cramped. Fetus sends out chemical signals to trigger labor. Not many babies are delivered on their due dates—some are early, some several weeks late. Doctors usually intervene once a baby is over two weeks later than expected, but the due date is only approximate. Unless a couple have had IVF, no one knows exactly when the sperm and the egg met—and time of ovulation varies. At the end of every pregnancy a baby is delivered and, for most people, this is a safe and happy event.

Biographies

Richard Howell

As an obstetrician and gynecologist, Richard Howell's job involves delivering babies and solving women's health issues. His main area of expertise is working with infertile couples, helping them to conceive and realize their dreams of becoming parents.

"I knew I wanted to enter this speciality the first time I saw a baby being born, when I was a medical student in London. For me it was the most beautiful sight, witnessing new life coming into the world and seeing the look of utter joy on the parents' faces. When I was doing my postgraduate training in London, IVF was in its early days and I wanted to become involved in this new and exciting area. Here was a branch of medicine where I could combine my inquiring scientific mind with clinical medicine and use my communication skills at the same time!"

Richard has had the pleasure of delivering many hundreds of the babies that were conceived as a result of infertility treatments in the hospitals and clinics where he has worked. These infertility treatments may involve the high-tech IVF or ICSI but are more commonly successful due to lifestyle changes. In each case, Richard works with couples to ensure both the woman and the man are in the best possible state of physical health to conceive, go through pregnancy without problems, and deliver a healthy baby safely into the world.

Ignaz Semmelweiss

In the late 18th and early 19th centuries, many mothers developed severe infections within days—or even hours—of giving birth in the maternity wards in hospitals. Childbed fever claimed the lives of about one woman in every five who gave birth. Charles White in the United Kingdom, and Oliver Wendell Holmes in the United States, tried to persuade people that it was doctors and nurses who were spreading the disease from patient to patient. Finally, Ignaz Phillipp Semmelweiss, a Hungarian physician, put together the evidence to prove it.

Semmelweiss worked at the Vienna General Hospital. The hospital maternity ward had one delivery room staffed by female midwives and another staffed by medical students. More than 12 percent of the women whose babies were delivered by the medical students died of fever—three times as many as those delivered in the other room. Semmelweiss realized that the medical students often went straight from performing an autopsy (dissecting a dead body) to delivering a baby without washing their hands. He wondered if they were carrying the cause of disease from the corpses to their patients in the maternity ward.

One day, a colleague cut himself while carrying out an autopsy and died shortly after from symptoms identical to those of childbed fever. For Semmelweiss this was the proof he needed. He insisted that his medical students wash their hands before they entered the maternity ward, and again between dealing with each patient. Within six months the mortality (death) rate of his patients had dropped by 75 percent. After two years, the mortality rate was down to only 1.27 percent of the women who gave birth to their babies in his wards.

When Semmelweiss became professor of obstetrics in Pest (now Budapest), he introduced antiseptic practices similar to those he had begun in Vienna. There, the number of women dying from childbed fever fell to 0.85 percent. Amazingly, other doctors rejected his findings—they didn't want to accept that they could be the cause of disease in their patients!

The scientists behind ultrasound scans

Ultrasound technology began as a technology for the military in the form of SONAR and RADAR—used by airplanes and submarines to locate approaching ships and aircraft.

It wasn't until the 1940s and 1950s that doctors started to use ultrasound to help heal people. In the United States in the late 1940s, scientists such as George Ludwig explored the use of ultrasound as a way of diagnosing problems inside the body. Ivan Greenwood was the engineer who made the first commercial "ultrasonic locator," and early uses of ultrasound scanning included diagnosing gallstones and kidney stones.

In the mid-1950s, teams of scientists and doctors in the United States and Japan began to explore the use of ultrasound scanning in many different medical conditions, including pregnancy.

Professor Ian Donald, from Glasgow University in Scotland, discovered—by accident—that when a pregnant patient had a full bladder it made it much easier to get good images of the fetus. Beginning in the mid-1960s, the use of ultrasound to measure the size of the head of the fetus became relatively common.

Find Out More

Books

Englander, Anrenée. *Dear Diary, I'm Pregnant*. Buffalo, N.Y.: Annick Press, 1997.

Fullick, Ann. *Science at the Edge: In Vitro Fertilization*. Chicago: Heinemann Library, 2009.

Harris, Robie, H. *Let's Talk About Girls, Boys, Babies, Bodies, Families, and Friends*. Cambridge, Mass.: Candlewick Books, 2006.

Harris, Robie, H. *Let's Talk About Where Babies Come From*. Cambridge, Mass.: Candlewick Books, 2004.

Meredith, Susan. *Growing Up (Facts of Life)*. Tulsa, Okla.: Usborne Books, 2004.

Websites

- www.mayoclinic.com/health/prenatal-care/PR00008
  Information about prenatal care in the United States.

- http://parenting.ivillage.com/pregnancy/calendar
  A personal pregnancy calendar that follows a baby's development from conception to delivery.

- www.4woman.gov/pregnancy
  The U.S. Department of Health & Human Services' website on pregnancy, childbirth, and beyond.

- www.pbs.org/wgbh/nova/miracle
  The companion website to Nova's "Life's Greatest Miracle" television series.

- www.wpclinic.org/parenting/fetal-development/first-trimester/
  Photographs of developing fetuses.

Topics for further study

- Ignaz Semmelweiss—the doctor who saved the lives of many women and babies when he discovered the importance of hand washing and hygiene in hospitals.

- Robert Edwards and Patrick Steptoe—the scientists who helped produce Louise Brown, the first baby born as a result of IVF.

- Dr. Ruben Quintero, Dr. Joe Bruner, and others involved in fetal surgery.

- Midwives—the women and men who, over the centuries, have carried out much of the care of women while they were pregnant, giving birth, and caring for a newborn baby.

- Fetal Alcohol Syndrome—research this condition and the effects that other drugs can have on the developing fetus.

- Prenatal care in your community, and around the world.

Glossary

allele   one of at least two alternative forms of a gene that you might inherit

amniotic fluid   protective fluid that surrounds the fetus

antibodies   blood protein that forms to fight against alien substances in the body, such as bacteria or a virus

asexual reproduction   one-parent reproduction, resulting in offspring identical to the parent

blastocyst   hollow ball of cells formed by about five days after the fertilization of the egg

Cesarean section   operation in which a baby is taken from the uterus out of an incision made through the abdominal wall and the uterus

carbon monoxide   poisonous gas found in cigarette smoke, which is carried in the blood of mothers who smoke and deprives the developing fetus of oxygen

colostrum   first milk produced by a mother after giving birth, which is very rich in antibodies

conceive   when an egg is fertilized and an embryo is created

contractions   pulsating movement made by the muscles of the uterus before and during labor

DNA (deoxyribonucleic acid)   chemical found in the nucleus of the cell, which makes up the chromosomes and carries the genetic code

embryo   offspring that is unborn and still in the process of development

enzymes   special proteins that make possible, or speed up, the rate of reaction

estrogen   female sex hormone made by the ovaries, involved in the development of the female sexual characteristics and the release of a mature egg in the menstrual cycle

fertility drugs   artificial hormones that may be used to trigger ovulation in infertile women

fetus developing human being after the first eight weeks of pregnancy

gametes   special sex cells involved in sexual reproduction. These are known as sperm and eggs in animals and humans, and as pollen and ovules in plants.

genes   units of inheritance

genetic diseases   diseases or conditions that occur due to inherited genes

genetic information   units of inheritance that are passed on in the genes from parents to offspring and determine the offspring's characteristics

genetic modification process by which the genetic material of a cell may be altered, either replacing damaged genetic material or adding extra genetic material

in vitro fertilization (IVF) infertility treatment in which eggs harvested from a woman are fertilized outside her body with sperm, allowed to develop for several days, and then placed into the uterus

labor process by which a baby is pushed out of the uterus, along with the placenta

lung surfactant chemical made in the lungs of the developing fetus, which makes it possible for the lungs to inflate when the first breath is drawn at birth

menopause end of a woman's reproductive life, when the levels of the sex hormones fall and there are no eggs left in the ovaries

midwives nurses who are specially qualified to provide prenatal care and to assist at births

miscarry when the baby dies and is lost from the body. Miscarriages sometimes happen because there is something wrong with the fetus, or with the way the woman's body reacts to pregnancy, but often the cause is unknown.

mutation tiny change in the DNA that can lead to a change in an inherited characteristic

ovulation release of a mature egg from the ovary

placenta organ that forms from both maternal and fetal tissue. It supplies the fetus with nutrients and oxygen and removes waste products.

puberty stage at which the body of a child undergoes physical development to become a sexually mature adult

pre-eclampsia complication that can occur during pregnancy, resulting in high blood pressure and other symptoms. It can pose a serious threat to mother and baby.

premature if a baby is born before 37 weeks of pregnancy

prenatal care care given to mother and fetus before the birth

semen mixture of sperm and fluids produced by a man when he ejaculates (discharges semen)

sexual reproduction two-parent reproduction, involving special sex cells known as gametes, which gives rise to offspring that are unique and different to their parents

terminate to end a pregnancy

testosterone male sex hormone that causes the development and maintenance of male sexual characteristics

uterus also known as the womb, this is where a fetus develops inside a female mammal

Index

alcohol **25**
alleles **29, 54**
amniocentesis **31, 49**
amniotic fluid **22, 24, 54**
antibodies **15, 18, 46, 54**
asexual reproduction **5, 54**

babies **44–7**
birds **6**
birth **32–5, 42, 49**
blastocyst **14, 48, 54**
blood transfusions **18**
bottle-feeding **46–7**
breast-feeding **46, 47**
Bruner, Dr. Joe **19**

Cesarean section **33, 49, 54**
carbon monoxide **27, 54**
cell division **14, 16, 30**
chorionic villus testing **31, 48**
chromosomes **28–9**
colostrum **46, 54**
conception (conceive) **12–14, 16, 36, 41, 54**
contractions **12, 19, 32, 54**
cystic fibrosis **30, 39**

death **4, 21, 24, 27, 50–1**
DNA **28–30, 54**
Down's syndrome **30, 31**
drugs **26–7, 33, 36, 39, 43, 48**

eggs **5–8, 10, 12–14, 28, 36–7, 39, 40, 42–3, 48**
embryo **5, 6, 14, 16, 24, 30, 39, 40–1, 48, 54**
enzymes **13, 54**
estrogen **10, 55**
ethical issues **40–3**

fallopian tubes **10, 12, 37, 38**
female reproductive system **10**
fertility drugs **36, 39, 43, 54**
fertility problems **36–43**
fertilization **13, 36, 37, 39, 42, 48**

fetus **9, 16–17, 24–7, 31, 32, 34, 42, 43, 48–9, 54**
fish **6**
folic acid **24**
food **24**
food poisoning **24**
formula **46–7**
frogs, strawberry poison **7**

gametes **5, 28, 54**
genes **29, 39, 54**
genetic diseases **30–1, 39, 41, 48, 49, 54**
genetic information **28–9, 54**
genetic modification **41, 54**

Harlow, Harry **45**
hormones **8, 10, 13, 14–15, 36, 39, 48**
Howell, Richard **50**

infertility **36–43**
in vitro fertilization (IVF) **39–43, 49, 50, 55**

kangaroos **6**

labor **23, 32–3, 34, 49, 55**
lung surfactant **34, 49, 55**

male reproductive system **9**
mammals **6**
marsupials **6**
menopause **10, 55**
menstrual cycle **13**
menstruation **10–11, 14, 48**
midwives **21, 50, 55**
milk **46–7**
miscarriage (miscarry) **16, 24, 27, 31, 55**
monkeys **45**
multiple births **36, 39, 42–3**
mutations **30, 55**

ovaries **10, 12, 36, 39, 48**
ovulation **13, 36, 46, 55**

pain relief **33**
periods **10–11, 14, 48**
placenta **14, 16, 25, 32, 42, 49, 55**
pre-eclampsia **20, 55**
pregnancy tests **15, 48**
premature babies **19, 27, 34, 35, 49, 55**
prenatal care **20–1, 22, 54**
puberty **8, 10–11, 55**

Quintero, Dr. Ruben **19**

reproduction **4–5**
reproductive system **9, 10**

semen **8, 9, 12, 38, 55**
Semmelweiss, Ignaz **50–1**
sexual reproduction **5, 8, 28, 55**
sexually transmitted diseases (STD) **37**
smoking **27, 36**
sperm **5, 6, 8–9, 12–14, 28, 37, 38–9, 41, 48**
spina bifida **19, 24**
stillbirth **27**
surgery, fetal **18–19**

termination **31, 55**
testes **8, 9, 39**
testosterone **8, 55**
thalidomide **26**
twins **18–19, 42**

ultrasound scans **18, 20, 39, 49, 51**
umbilical cord **18**
uterus **10, 12–14, 16, 20, 24, 32, 37, 39, 48, 55**

zygote **14, 42**